TAMBOUR EMBROIDERY FOR BEGINNERS

A Simple Guide To Learn About Tambour Embroidery, Tambour Hook, With Various Steps.

Copyright@2023

Jane Roland

Table Of Content

Chapter One

   A Short Overview of Tambour

Chapter Two

   Lesson On Tambour Embroidery

   What supplies are required for embroidering tambour?

   Weaving a Chain

Chapter Three

   Tambour beading and bead embroidery

   Materials

   Fixing the frame in place

   Simple Tambour Stitch

Chapter Four

   Weaving a tambour

   Sequins

   The Embroidered Hummingbird

Chapter Five

   First Class in Tambour Lace

   Materials Required:

Chapter One

A Short Overview of Tambour

Embroideries from as early as the 16th century provide evidence of the long history of tambour beading. It originated in Asia, but by the 18th century, it had made its way to Europe, where it was first mentioned. All of the best tambour beadwork ever created came to France and England by way of India, Persia, and China.

780–95 Craft of French Tambour Embroidery

The drum-shaped frame initially employed in tambour beadwork gave rise to the name: "tambour" is the French word for drum. Since it was something new and interesting, it quickly gained popularity among women.

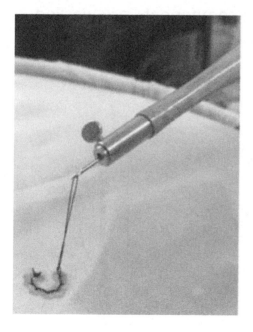

Tambour embroidery requires simply a single basic stitch. A

fine, pointed hook is used in place of a needle to pierce through tightly stretched cloth, catching and drawing up a beaded, fine thread from below to form a connected, chain-like stitch. The pattern is built up from the underside of the cloth as the components are worked on from the back.

Finely Beaded Tambour for High Fashion

Because it's a continuous stitch, embroidery can now be done considerably more quickly than with conventional beadwork. Even without embellishments like beads or sequins, the method may be employed to lovely effect.

Tambourwork's meteoric rise to fame in the 18th century was followed by a rocky ride into the 19th, when new machines were created that could achieve the same results far more quickly than by hand.

Chanel Haute Couture Fall/Winter 2014

However, tambour beading is still commonly utilized today,

particularly in high-end fashion where only the best decorated items would do.

We offer lessons for beginners all the way up to advanced tambour beading techniques!

Chapter Two

Lesson On Tambour Embroidery

The tambourine (a kind of drum) inspired the term »Tambour Embroidery. For the purpose of this kind of embroidery, cloth is drum-tight stretched into a frame. Famous French couture needlework houses like »Lesage« use this technique. This method is also known as

»Lunéville« in its native France. When compared to traditional stitching techniques, tambour embroidery allows for fundamentally quicker growth with just a few hours of practice. This article provides a straightforward, step-by-step method to completing this age-old kind of needlework.

What supplies are required for embroidering tambour?

Tambourine needles are very sharp and thin crochet needles. Be sure the needle's opening is facing the same direction as the locking screw before inserting it. This facilitates evaluation of the crochet's directional orientation throughout the embroidery process. If you're just starting out with tambour, I recommend taking some time to experiment with various stitching and textile embellishment methods on a scrap of cloth. Tulle might work, but organza is preferable. In theory, if you have a steady touch with the needle, you might adapt this kind of needlework to various fabrics. Threads like »Fil a Gant,« silk thread, embroidery twist, and metallic thread are all good options. To get started, try your hand at the classic chain stitch in a range of sizes. After that, you may experiment with circular embroidery, surface embroidery, and gorgeous corners. Finally, you may embellish it with beads or sequins. Tambourine needlework does not require the use of either hand, hence a unique embroidery hoop may be utilized.

Fastening the first part of the seam

First, We begin by demonstrating how to repair the seam's initial formation. The stitch is worked a little bigger than required to provide a clearer example. The fastening stitches should be as tiny as possible so as not to draw undue attention to themselves.

To hold the embroidery thread beneath the embroidery frame, first wrap it around your index finger and then secure it with your thumb on your middle finger.

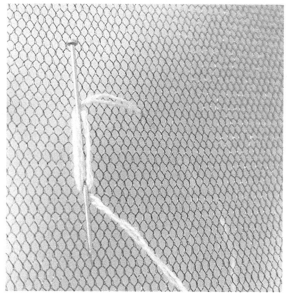

Second, Grab the yarn's

beginning and prick it with the tambourine needle from above. Set the needle beside the yarn and secure the beginning by winding it three times around the needle.

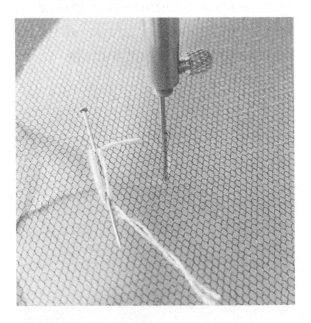

Third, The needle is inserted from above, some distance from the thread's origin, to create the initial stitch. Needles always open toward the direction of stitching (in this example, right) and their locking screws are turned clockwise. Needle threading is made easier when the needle is held as upright as feasible.

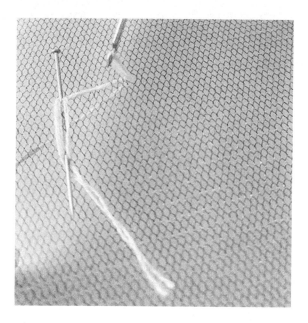

Four, Turn the needle 180 degrees counterclockwise, so that the screw and the aperture are facing left, then wrap the yarn once around the whole needle from behind. Pull the yarn gently with your fingers to raise the tension and stabilize the yarn in the needle hook. The trail can at last be exposed. The thread tension may be loosened once again in preparation for the next stitch.

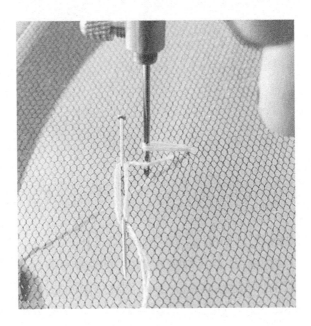

Fifth, The needle is in the right place to start a reverse stitch that will finish behind the first one.

o

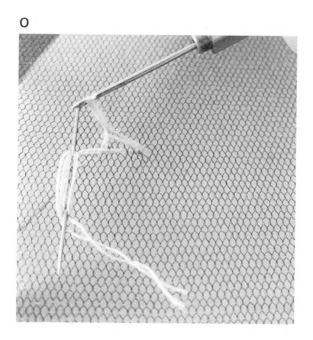

Six, after you've completed the reverse stitch, you'll need to wound the thread around the needle again, turn it 180 degrees, secure the thread in the hook, and draw it to the surface so that the loop passes through the previous stitch.

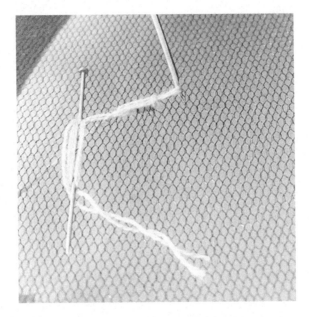

Seven, The older loop gets dragged along with the newer one when the latter is tugged to the right. Now, tighten the previous loop by drawing the thread beneath the embroidery hoop.

Eight, The last safety stitch, number three, is positioned behind the first stitch. Once the needle is in place, the yarn is looped around the crochet a second time before the work is rotated around 180 degrees and the loop is pulled up.

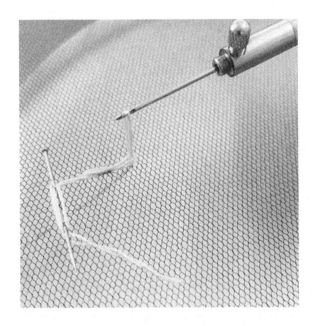

Nine, The seam is now secure, and the embroidery proper may begin, after these three stages (insertion, back stitch, forward stitch).

Weaving a Chain

The chain stitch may be used to create straight lines or to fill up large spaces. All stitches are worked forward, but the idea is the same as with the securing stitch.

Chapter Three

Tambour beading and bead embroidery

The stunning embroidery patterns seen at haute couture fashion shows are a combination of thread, sequins, and beads to create amazing, intricate motifs used to adorn evening dresses, collars, and cuffs. The elaborate designs used in haute couture are usually drawn by hand. Beadwork and threadwork may be so detailed that whole skirts are covered with them. The construction of one of them is mysterious.

Tambour embroidery is often the correct response. A tambour hook, which is similar in shape to a sharp crochet hook, is used to create tambour needlework. You can almost see through the cloth as you work with the hook. Beads and sequins may be threaded onto the yarn and worked into the spaces between the "hookings" to create continuous strands.

Both sides of the cloth will be needed. The tambour hook is driven through the cloth from one side, and the thread is wrapped around it from the opposite side using the other hand. When the thread is reversed, the hook catches it and the stitch is tightened by pulling the thread between the cloth and the prior stitch. When working with beads, the design is created on the "wrong side" of the cloth. For this reason, it is preferable to work on top of a translucent fabric, such as silk organza.

Having sewed beads onto an article of clothing once, I knew there was nothing particularly remarkable about tambour beading, but I couldn't see how it might be utilized for putting different beads that are not in tidy rows. A needle small enough to pass through your beads' openings is all you'll need.

I decided to use all of these methods together to make one simple pattern. However, let's start with the supplies.

Materials

Here is a quick rundown of the supplies I tapped into:

- Tambourine Hook

- Silk Organza

- Frame (I repurposed a bit of a silk painting frame)

- a stapler and staples

- cotton twill tape

- embroidery thread

- buttonhole twist and a stapler

- 3 or 4 centimeters in width

- Beads, sequins, pins, needles (including some small ones to fit through the holes in your beads), normal polyester sewing thread

Fixing the frame in place

As I said, I adapted the frame of one of my silk paintings. Even though I couldn't get the frame's sides to be perfectly parallel, it nevertheless served its purpose.

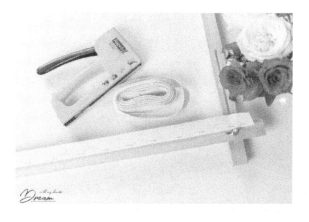

A scrap of silk organza was lying around, so I used it to make a rectangle. I attached twill tape to two of the frame's sides with staples so that I could hang my silk. Once I had the twill tape in place, I was able to baste my silk organza to it.

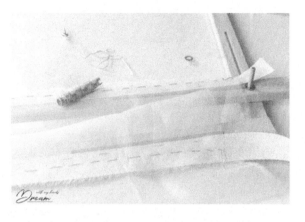

You may use any sort of thread; I used silk buttonhole twist; however, a stronger thread would be preferable. You may use regular topstitching thread successfully.

The fabric was then pulled taut over the skeleton. Wrapping twill tape around the two ends of the frame served as a mounting point for the sides:

Simple Tambour Stitch

The fundamental stitch, including the "away" and "towards" directions, must be mastered first. When changing directions, I found that wrapping the thread and rotating the hook needed to be done in the other way. First, I constructed a leaf and a floral stem out of gold DMC Cotton Perle thread.

To determine exactly where the hook is, line it up with the screw on the holder. With the hook oriented in the direction you want to go, you may easily pierce through the cloth. After that, you'll wrap the thread counterclockwise around the hook (if you're facing away from you). Then, counter-clockwise flip the hook 180 degrees and re-enter the cloth, extending the hole with the rear of the hook to ensure a smooth passage. You'll coil the thread and spin the hook clockwise as you reverse course and come back closer yourself.

Afterwards, I gave Raiman Rayon Machine Embroidery Thread a go and attempted to embroider a flower.

The finished product looked great with the cotton perle thread. The impression created by the machine embroidery thread, however, was a little too weak and thin. If you're trying to sew on beads, regular thread from your sewing machine will do the job just as well.

The chain stitch develops on the side opposite to where the hook is being used. A single row of stitches may be seen on the reverse:

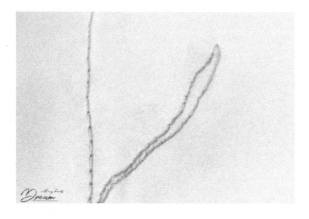

Whichever side you wish to utilize is OK. If you'd rather work with the back of the cloth against the frame, you may do that, too.

Chapter Four

Weaving a tambour

The beads vary in thickness from 2-3 mm, and I have some in bright yellow, orange, and red. When starting a tambour beading project, the beads must be placed in the tread. To attach the beads to the thread, I made use of a very fine needle. Following the instructions in one of the tutorials, I brought the beginning thread to the wrong side and stitched it in place. After that, I set out to create the string of beads.

If you are right-handed, the beading will be done with your left hand. Simply insert your needle through the fabric, press a bead into position with your left hand, and secure it with a wrap of thread around the hook. The last step of the stitch is completed in the same manner as the first.

From the perspective of the employee, the job appears like this:

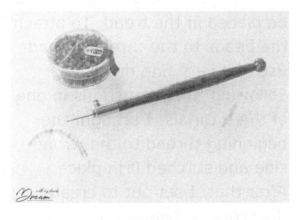

On the "right" side, a similar string of beads is formed:

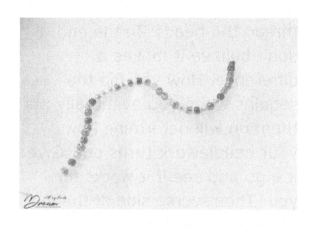

Sequins

Sequins may be thought of as flat beads. You may stack them as I did, or you can arrange them next to each other. At first, I wasn't really sure how to thread the beads. In the end, I don't believe it makes a difference. How you flip the sequins when you eventually put them on will determine how your needlework turns out. Give it a go and see if it works for you. The reverse side of the sequins looks like this:

The Embroidered Hummingbird

Even after hours of searching online, I couldn't locate a pattern I liked. After much deliberation, I settled on this image of an embroidered hummingbird from the internet, which I can no longer access. Then, I used an erasable marker to transfer my design from the printed out version onto the silk. Then I traced it with a tambour hook and stitched it in place.

I had a large variety of beads and sequins on hand, and I played around with several color schemes and bead placements until I was satisfied. Since I couldn't string together more jewels in a single row, I resorted to a different kind of stitching.

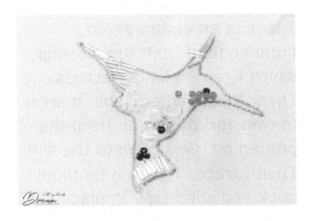

I began with the hummingbird's tail and worked my way around the design, adding cotton perle stitches for definition and satin stitches for shine. Even though my colors were totally off and I used beads instead of regular embroidery thread, I did my best to replicate the original picture's color patterns. I'm pleased with the outcome of this little guy. I was thinking of sewing a matching set in reverse so that I could appliqué them together. Once I've gotten some more skill with tambour beading, I plan on making a small, beaded pocketbook.

New information is usually exciting. I just had to go out and get the hook; the rest of the stuff I already had lying around the house. I thought it would be a lot messier than it turned out to be. The photographs simply don't do justice to my tiny hummingbird. It was challenging for me to capture the light's reflection off of the beads and sequins.

Chapter Five

First Class in Tambour Lace

The response to my latest Tambour project has been encouraging, so I've decided to provide additional tutorials. It's not something I can accomplish in one sitting.

Since my current primary usage for tambour is in lace, it is what I want to teach first. Though I may add to this later on when I finish other projects, the methods shown here apply just as well to weaving.

Some background: An ancient Indian art style, tambour decoration first appeared in Europe in the middle of the 1700s, thanks to the popularity of tambour-embroidered fabrics.

Originally an imported craft, at the end of the 18th century making tambour was a favorite leisure for affluent ladies. It was particularly admired as an addition to the flimsy gowns of the 1790s and early 1800s. Until the 1840s, when machine-made lace started to take control, tambour lace was still widely used.

I'm going to teach you the fundamentals in three easy stages today:

The first step is to gather your supplies and begin weaving.

Second step, Tambourine stitch,

Third Step, concluding the thread.

Materials Required:

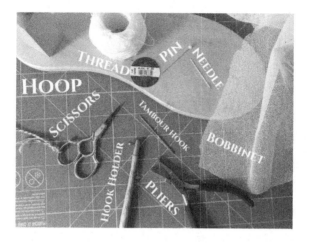

- An independent hoop or frame for embroidering. Images showing women making tambour at home often include round frames, whereas those of professionals using huge, rectangular frames are more common. You may sit on the ground, a table, or even your lap, but you must be able to use both hands.

- There are a variety of sizes of tambour hooks and tambour needles to accommodate different types of cloth and thread. I'm pretty sure the one I'm using in this article is a #90, but to be honest, I tossed it into the holder years ago and haven't looked at it since. Varieties with and without a latch are available. I prefer not to have one, but if you're having difficulties keeping your grip without one, by all means try it out!

- To keep your hook handy as you work, you'll need a "hook holder," sometimes known as the wooden handle.

- Fabric—I often work lace on cotton bobbinet, but silk net, muslin, linen, silk chiffon, and other textiles are all fair game. Tulle from a discount fabric shop is not a good choice for making tambour. The rule of "buy cheap, work up to the expensive" does not apply here. The basic synthetic tulle will snag on the hook and cause you to tear out your hair in no time. Don't automatically dismiss tambour because of one bad encounter with synthetic tulle.

• Thread; any strong, uncut thread will do; embroidery floss is not recommended. I'm working with a size 70 DMC Cordonnet Special. These embroidery threads are great because they have a wonderful sheen and produce sturdy, even stitches. Plain Gütermann 100% cotton sewing thread is what I go for when I need something extremely delicate to fill in themes.

• Cutters, Needles, Pins, and Scissors

• A pair of pliers is helpful but not required.

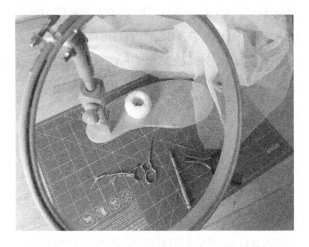

Both a lap frame, like the one shown in the instructional image above, and a freestanding tambour frame are available for purchase on this website. Hooks and holders are available. All of these goods may be found elsewhere if you do some searching, although you'll likely find the identical stuff offered by various stores.

PART 1: Gather your supplies.

Put the hook into the holder and screw it securely. Keep the hook pointing in the same direction as the screw so you can tell which way the hook is pointing without looking at it. This is crucial information. Keeping the hook small makes it easier to manipulate. My own is protruding approximately 1 1/2 inches from its holder.

Before you put your fabric in the hoop, you'll need to transfer your design onto it. I did not sketch a pattern in order to focus on teaching the stitch, but I will go into more depth about this in subsequent instructions on following a design. When I'm not doing public demonstrations in historical clothing, I mark designs with a blue water-soluble fabric marker. (Before using your marker on the whole piece of cloth, try a small area to make sure it washes off). Instead, I use pencil, which usually disappears after a few rubs, or I baste over the pattern with very fine white thread that will be covered up when the piece is done.

Prepare your hoop by inserting your fabric. First, tighten the screw until everything is secure, then pull the cloth as taut as possible. Repeat this process until you can pull the cloth as taut as possible and the hoop screw will not go any farther. At the very end, I use a set of pliers to make sure it's as secure as it can be. Since a drum head requires taut fabric, the term "tambour" is used to describe this craft. When the cloth is removed from the hoop, this prevents the stitches from puckering.

PART 2: Fasten the thread.

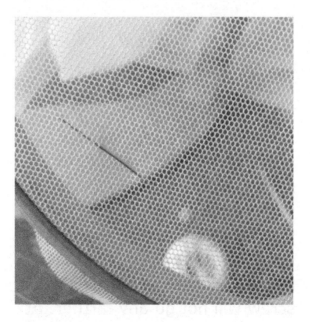

Pin the backing of your cloth to the floor several inches away from where you want to start embroidering.

Wrap the thread's end around the pin multiple times from the wrong side of the cloth, and you should be good to go. Do not disconnect the thread's working end from the spool. When working tambour, the thread shouldn't need to be cut till the very end.

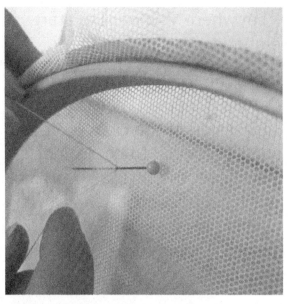
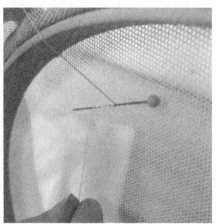

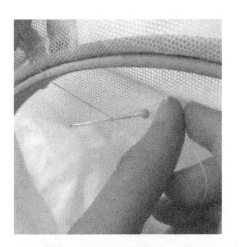
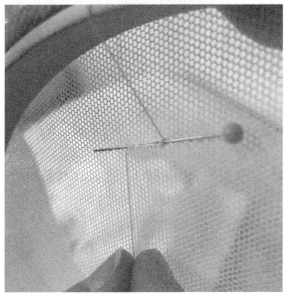

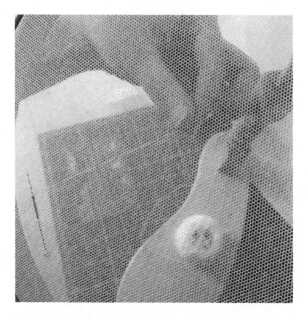

PART 3: Stitching Basics

Please read this full procedure many times before doing it on your own. Having a complete understanding of everything before getting started is crucial.

Put your non-dominant hand under the cloth to steady the thread. Use your dominant hand to poke a hole for the hook in the cloth. The direction of travel should be indicated by the orientation of the hook. You should position the handle so that it is about perpendicular to the cloth.

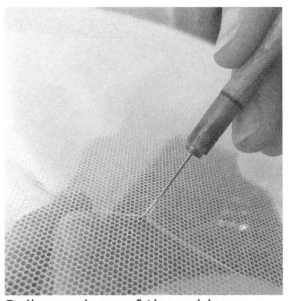

Pull up a loop of thread by wrapping it around the hook and rotating it so that the pointy end faces away from the direction in which you want to stitch (in this example, the hook is looking straight towards the camera, and I wish to stitch along the line directly away from the camera). You need to turn the hook around so that it is pointing in the direction you wish to go.

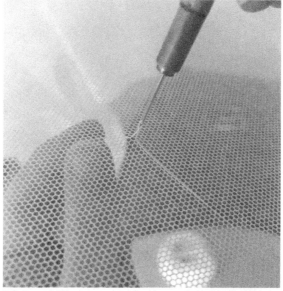

This will prevent the thread from slipping off of the hook as you go to the next stitch.

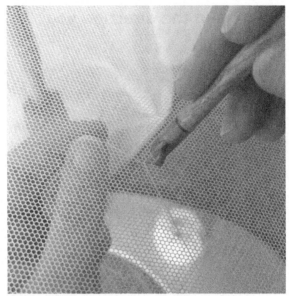

Place the hook into the next available net cell along the embroidering line. Don't be discouraged if you have to start again a few times after dropping this first major stitch.

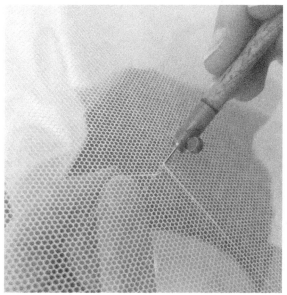

When wrapping the thread around the hook, rotate it counterclockwise so that it catches in the hook as you reel it up.

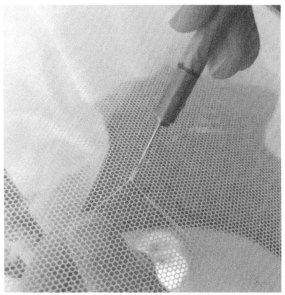

With the new thread wrap pulled up and through the first loop, bring the hook back up. When this occurs, the hook must be turned such that it points in the direction of the previous stitch. As a result, the hook may move freely around the chain without becoming caught in the loop. If you push the holder in the direction the hook will go, the rear of the hook will press softly against the net, easing its passage through the cloth. If you do this, the hook will have more space to pass through the cloth without becoming caught.

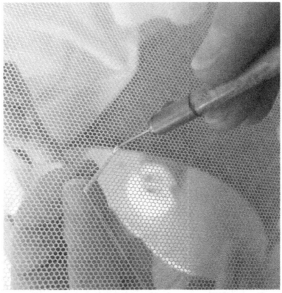

To finish making the traditional tambour chain stitch, proceed as before

i . Turn the hook so that it points in the desired direction.

i i. Put the hook through the cloth.

i i i. Wind the thread around the hook and turn it so that the eye is facing the already-made stitches.

iv. Raise the new thread loop above the previous thread loop and fabric.

In the Book, It can be seen wrapping the thread and turning the hook in a clockwise motion. When you do them both in the same direction, the thread slides more easily into the hook. To prepare the thread for the next stitch, I "unrotate" the hook by turning it counterclockwise above the cloth.

Don't freak out if you lose the thread or pull your hook out of the loop by mistake. You may just loop it back around and go on to the next cell. However, the whole project may come undone if the working thread is pulled before the hook has passed through the last loop. If you make a mistake in the pattern, you may easily remedy it by pulling the thread until the error disappears, then reattaching your hook to the free loop and continuing the design. However, things go downhill quickly if you've finally mastered the technique and thens rip out all of your carefully chained threads.

Once you've mastered the mechanics of making the stitch, tension should become your primary concern. When embroidering, if the thread is not held tight with the non-dominant hand, the stitches will be sloppy and loose after the hoop tension is relaxed. If you grip it too hard, you risk pulling the stitches too tightly and creating puckers in the cloth. Maintain your concentration on gently guiding the thread under the cloth with your thumb and finger. When you draw out the bobbin thread on a sewing machine, you feel a mild, malleable strain.

Part 4: wrap up the thread.

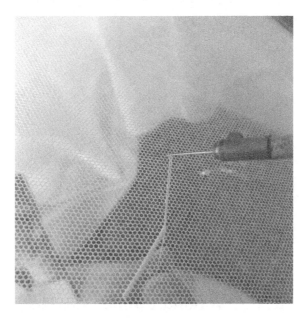

When you're done with your pattern, leave the last loop lengthy. This prevents the work from coming undone when you flip the hoop and snip the thread in use.

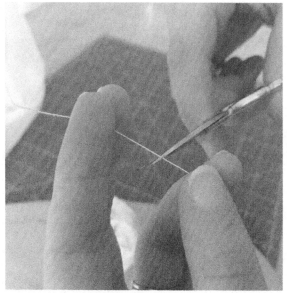

Raise the embroidery hoop and cut the working thread, leaving a long enough tail to thread the needle.

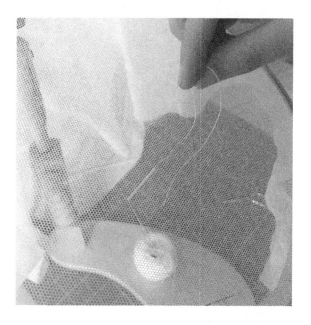

Turn the embroidery hoop around so the front is facing you, and draw the long loop until the thread's end pokes through the top of the cloth.

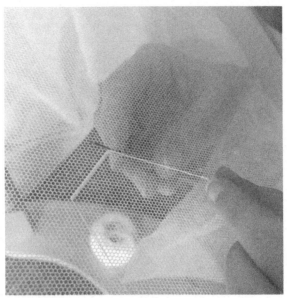

A thread end will be poking through the center of your last stitch. You'll want to bring your hook up through the cloth in the same cell as your last stitch, but you don't want to go through the stitch itself.

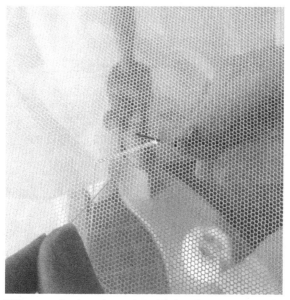

Thread the hook with the end of your thread. After that, you need to yank the thread's tail back to the underside of your project. Despite appearances, this is all that is required to prevent the sutures from coming undone.

Part 5: weave in the loose ends.

Do it as you go; trust me on this. How am I aware of this? Because weaving in ends is BOOOOOORING and I usually want to put it off until the conclusion of a project, I often don't do it until then. If you leave twenty or more ends till the conclusion of a project, you'll have to spend hours weaving them in all at once, which is really tedious. Take note of my blunders. Doing things as you go is a much better option. A single tambour motif, or potentially more, can be created with just two ends of thread if you are skilled at planning the course for your pattern. In subsequent guides, I'll demonstrate how to seamlessly transition from one section to the next without breaking the thread.

Next up: tying up loose ends.

Put one of the tails into the eye of a needle. Your work's reverse side should resemble a row of tiny back stitches or machine stitches. The needle should be inserted into and pulled through one of these stitches. The next "back-stitch" is where the needle will be inserted and pulled through. Keep going until the thread is fairly secure, or for at least an inch or two. I just did about a half an inch since this line is so short. The right side of your chain stitch may pucker if you pull these threads too tightly. You may use a hook instead of a needle to weave in the ends, but I think that using a needle is much quicker.

Trim the thread that is hanging out of the project in the same way.

Made in the USA
Monee, IL
12 August 2023